Warming Up for Viola

book one

by Cassia Harvey

Edited by Judith Harvey

This book was written as a study book for a class setting, but can also be played as part of individual study. Less-advanced (A) pages are structured so that they can be played together with more-advanced (B) pages. This allows less-advanced students to play in the same class as more-advanced students.

If you are playing this book as an individual, try playing all of the (A) pages first and then, starting from the beginning, play the (B) pages.

Supplemental shifting books, such as Third Position for the Viola, Book One (CHP214) are recommended before studying the (B) pages in this book.

CHP119
©2004 by C. Harvey Publications® All Rights Reserved.
www.charveypublications.com - print books and free sheet music blog
www.learnstrings.com - PDF downloadable books and chamber music

Contents

Page

G Major

2	Daily Exercise (A)
3	March (A)
4	Daily Exercise (B)
5	March (B)
6	Finger Workout (A)
7	Sonata (A)
8	Finger Workout (B)
9	Sonata (B)
10	Finger Twister (A)
11	Dill Pickle Rag (A)
12	Finger Twister (B)
13	Dill Pickle Rag (B)

D Major

14	Daily Exercise (A)
15	Variations on a Theme (A)
16	Daily Exercise (B)
17	Variations on a Theme (B)
18	Finger Workout (A)
19	Rondo (A)
20	Finger Workout (B)
21	Rondo (B)
22	Finger Twister (A)
23	Miss Ratray's Reel (A)
24	Finger Twister (B)
25	Miss Ratray's Reel (B)

C Major

26	Daily Exercise (A)
27	Mason's Apron (A)
28	Daily Exercise (B)
29	Mason's Apron (B)
30	Finger Workout (A)
31	Bourree (A)
32	Finger Workout (B)
33	Bourree (B)
34	Finger Twister (A)
35	Grazioso (A)
36	Finger Twister (B)
37	Grazioso (B)

F Major

38	Daily Exercise (A)
39	Variation (A)
40	Daily Exercise (B)
41	Variation (B)
42	Finger Workout (A)
43	Allegro (A)
44	Finger Workout (B)
45	Allegro (B)
46	Finger Twister (A)
47	The Dashing Sergeant (A)
48	Finger Twister (B)
49	The Dashing Sergeant (B)

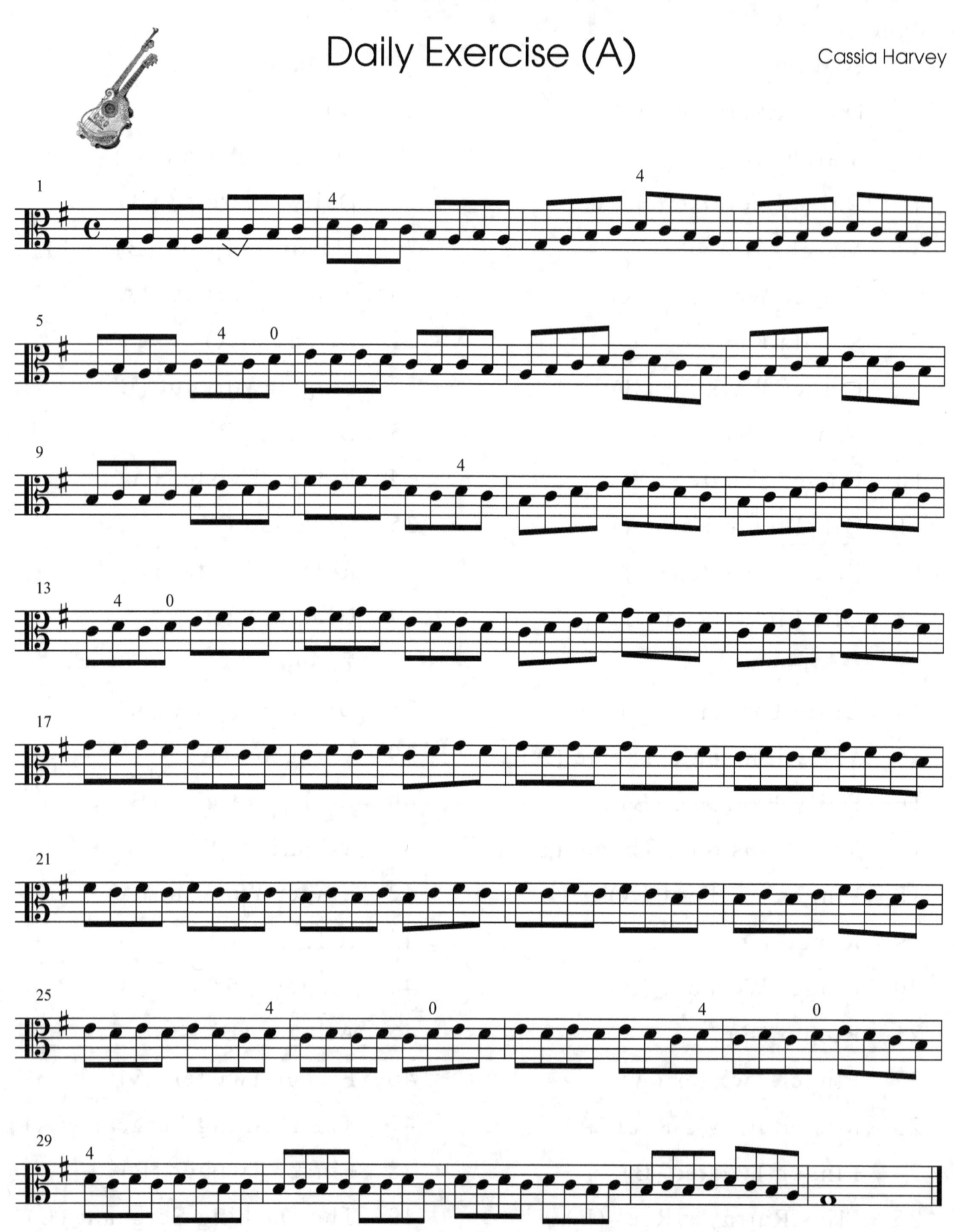

March (A)

L. Mozart, arr. Harvey

©2004 C. Harvey Publications All Rights Reserved.

Warming Up for Viola, Book One

Daily Exercise (B)

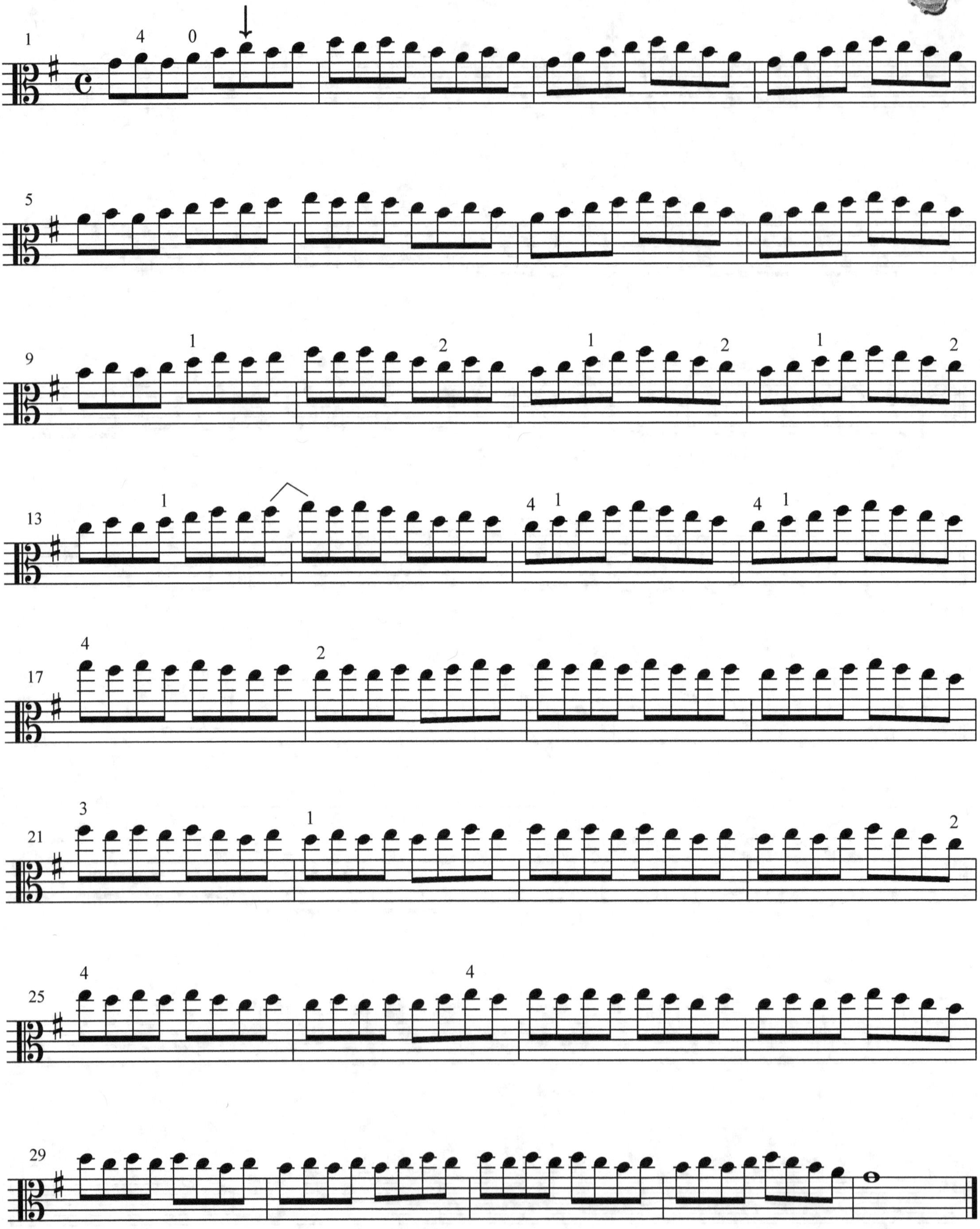

March (B)

L. Mozart, arr. Harvey

Finger Workout (A)

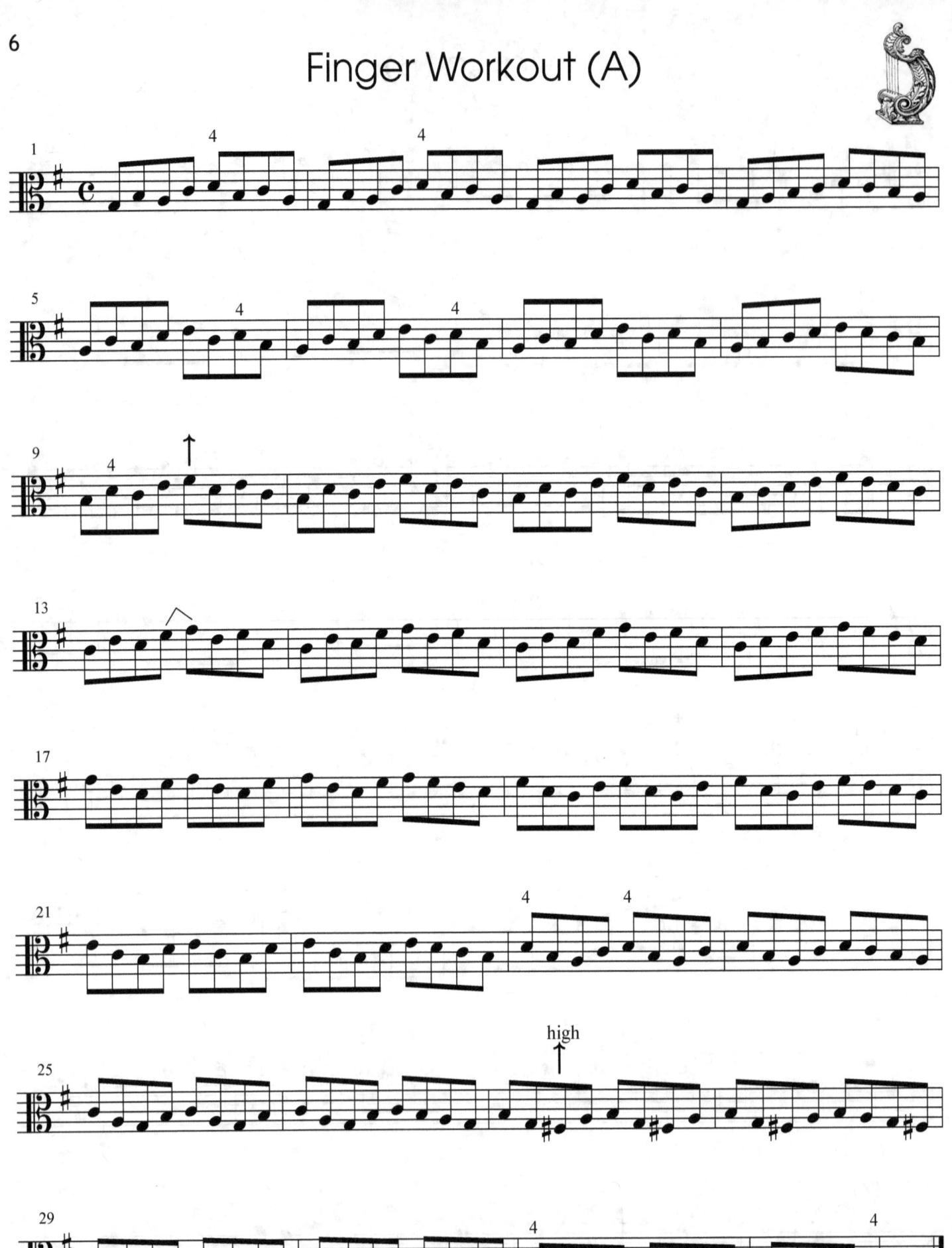

Warming Up for Viola, Book One ©2004 C. Harvey Publications All Rights Reserved.

Sonata (A)

Cimarosa, arr. Harvey

Warming Up for Viola, Book One

Finger Workout (B)

Sonata (B)

Cimarosa, arr. Harvey

Finger Twister (A)

Dill Pickle Rag (A)

Johnson, arr. Harvey

Finger Twister (B)

Dill Pickle Rag (B)

Johnson, arr. Harvey

Warmups in D major
Daily Exercise (A)

Variations on a Theme (A)

Romberg, arr. Harvey

Daily Exercise (B)

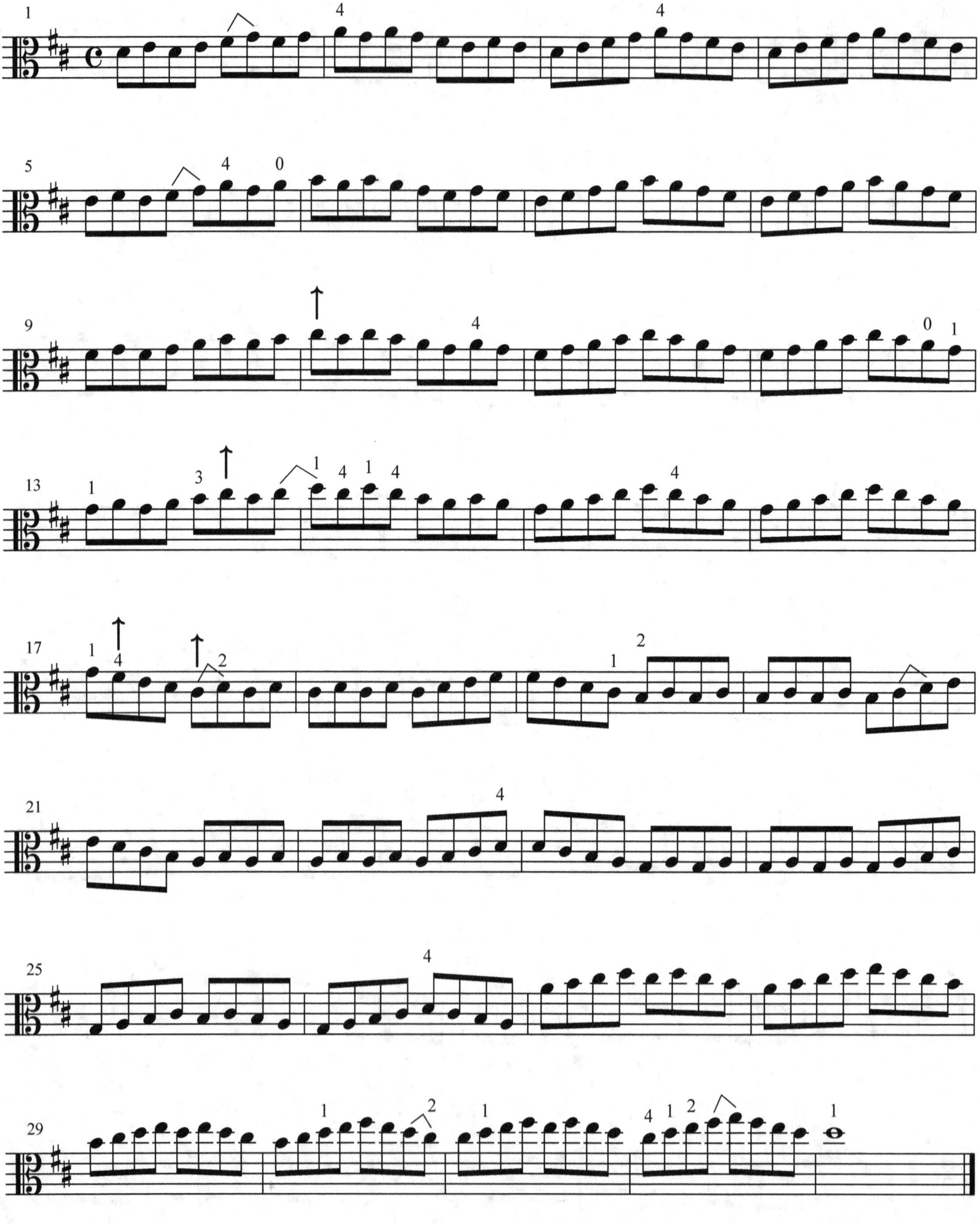

Variations on a Theme (B)

Romberg, arr. Harvey

©2004 C. Harvey Publications All Rights Reserved.

Warming Up for Viola, Book One

Finger Workout (A)

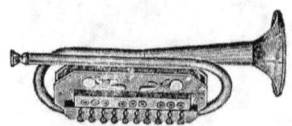

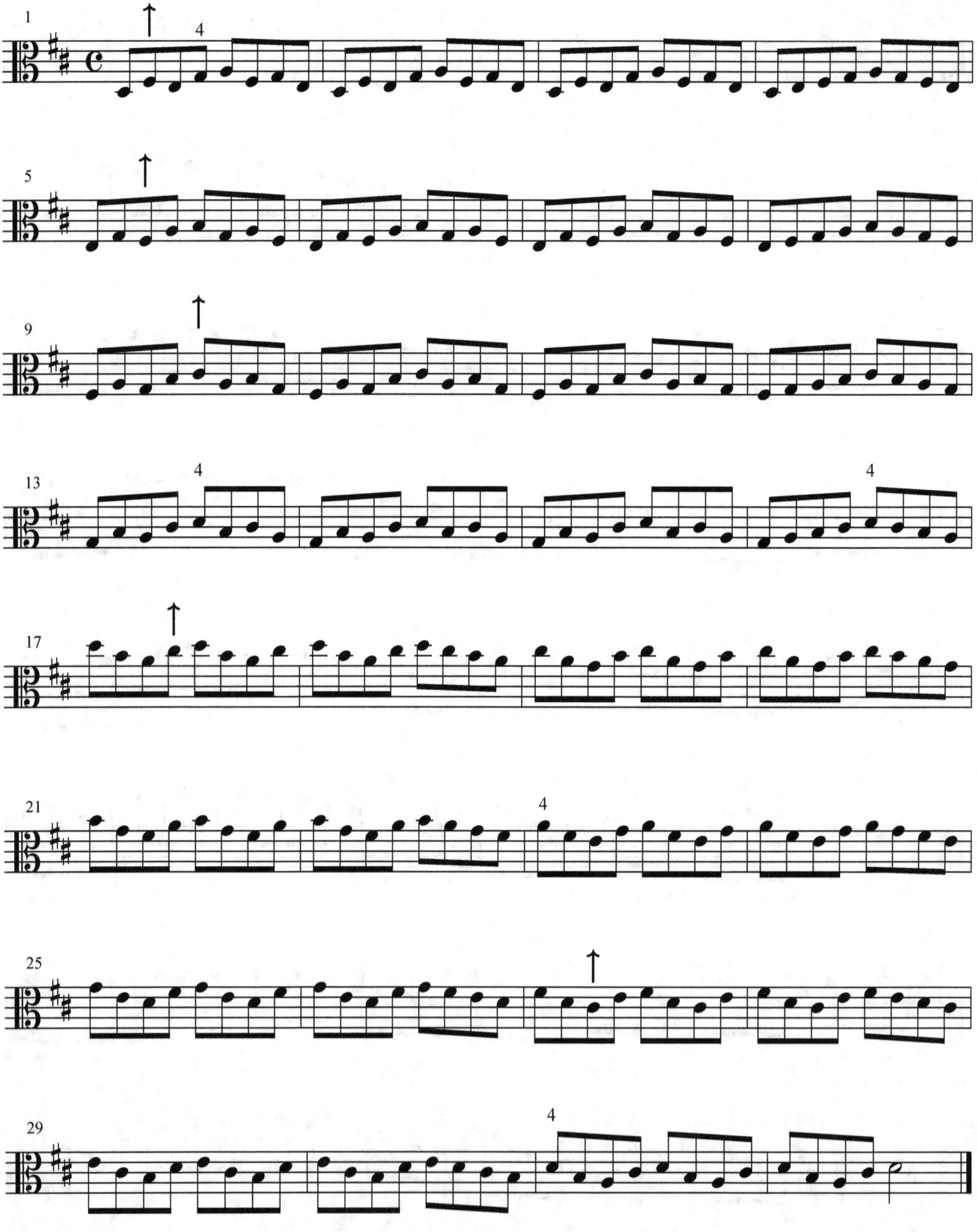

Rondo (A)

Mozart, arr. Harvey

©2004 C. Harvey Publications All Rights Reserved.

Warming Up for Viola, Book One

Finger Workout (B)

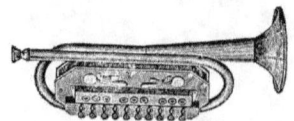

Rondo (B)

Mozart, arr. Harvey

Finger Twister (A)

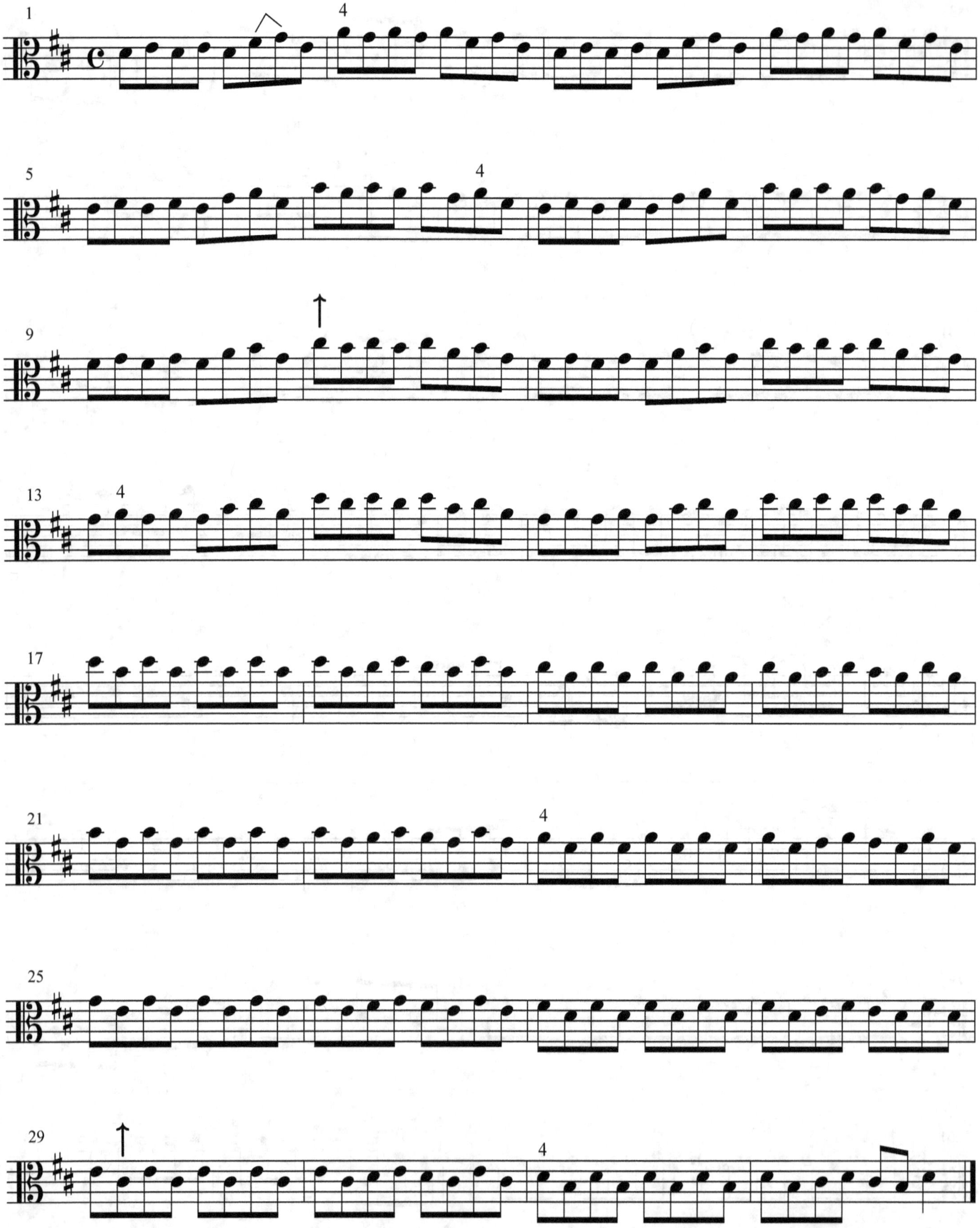

Miss Ratray's Reel (A)

Trad., arr. Harvey

Finger Twister (B)

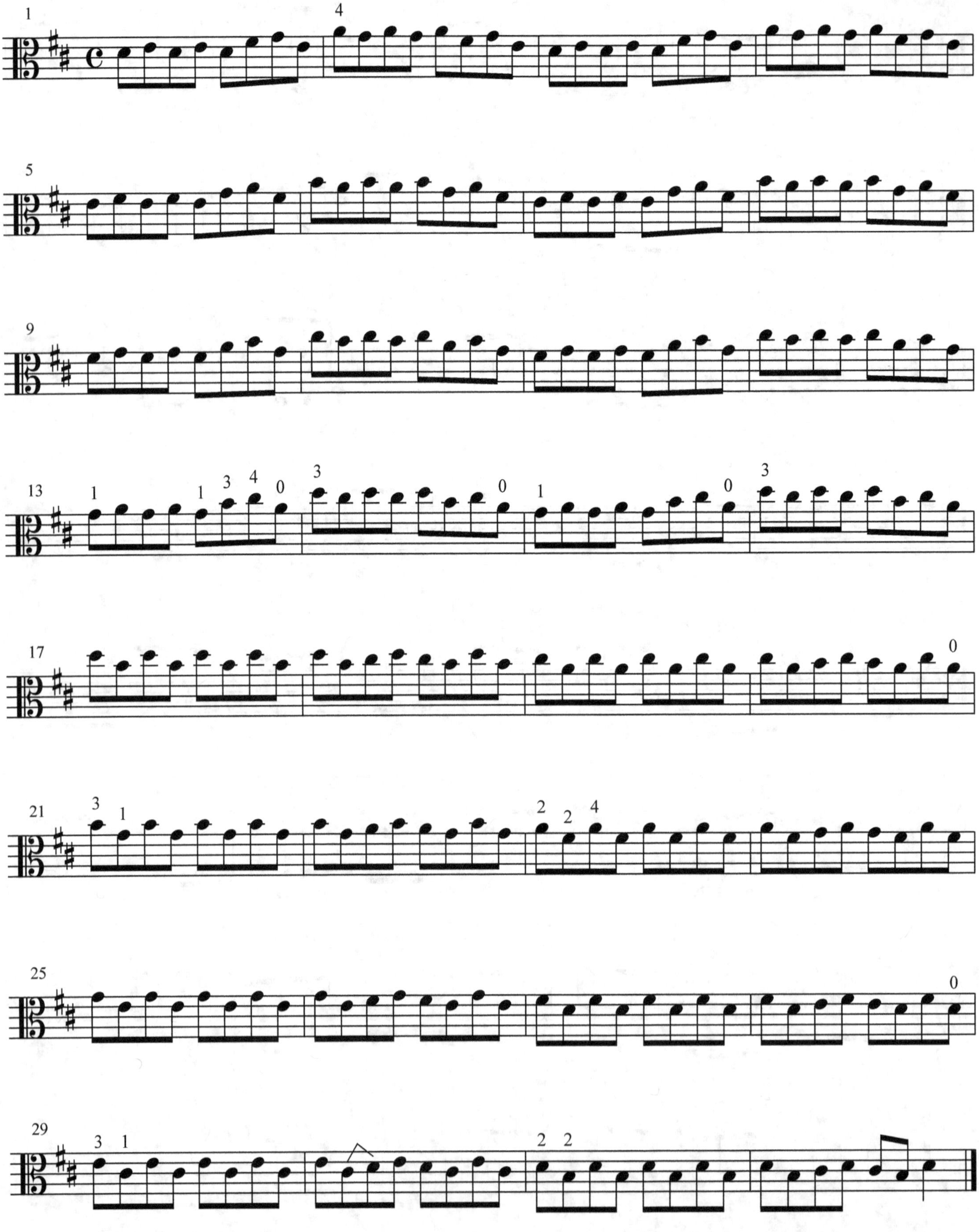

Miss Ratray's Reel (B)

Trad., arr. Harvey

Warming Up for Viola, Book One

Warmups in C major
Daily Exercise (A)

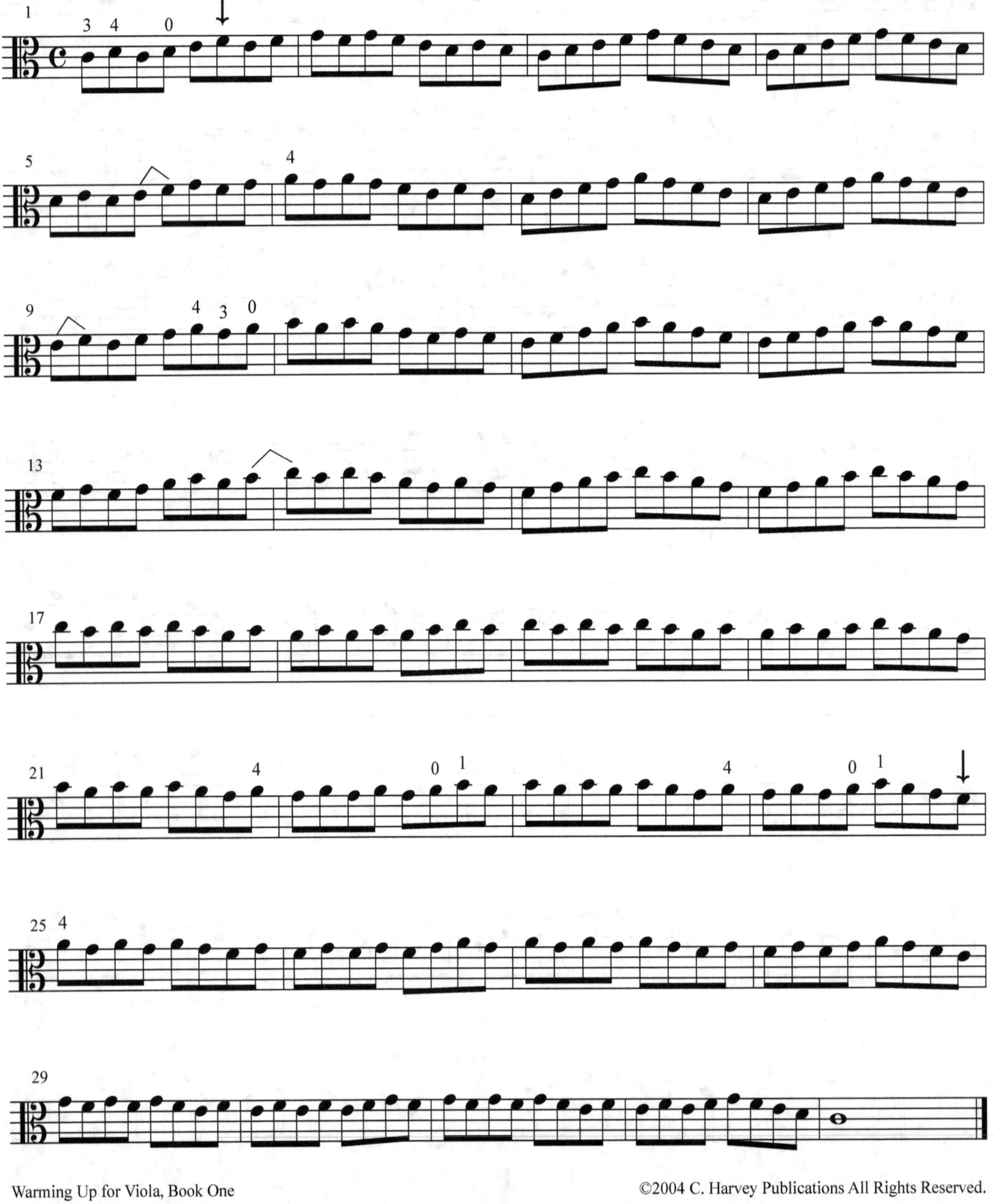

Mason's Apron (A)

Trad., arr. Harvey

Daily Exercise (B)

Mason's Apron (B)

Trad., arr. Harvey

Finger Workout (A)

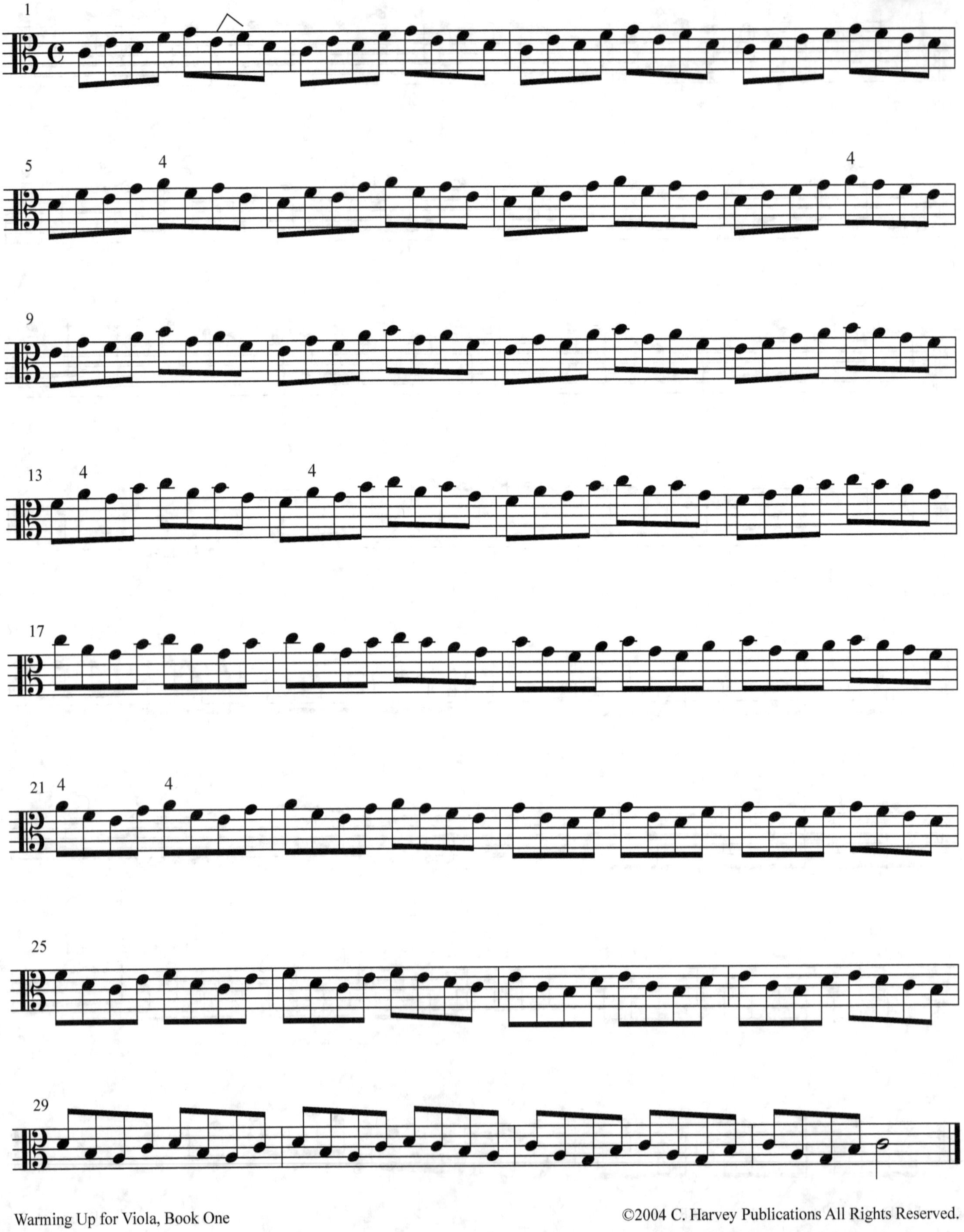

Bourree (A)

Bach, arr. Harvey

Finger Workout (B)

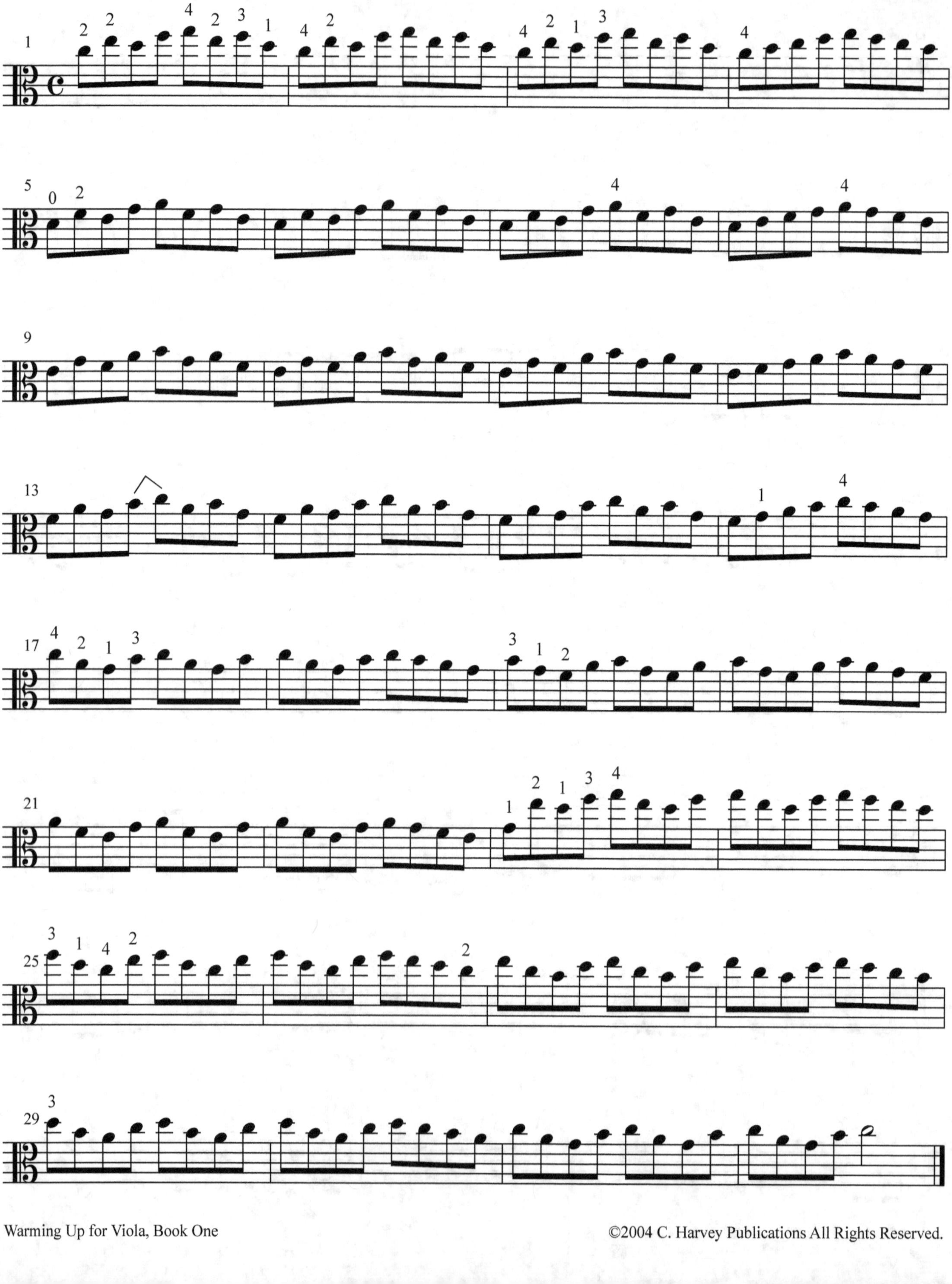

Bourree (B)

Bach, arr. Harvey

©2004 C. Harvey Publications All Rights Reserved.

Warming Up for Viola, Book One

Finger Twister (A)

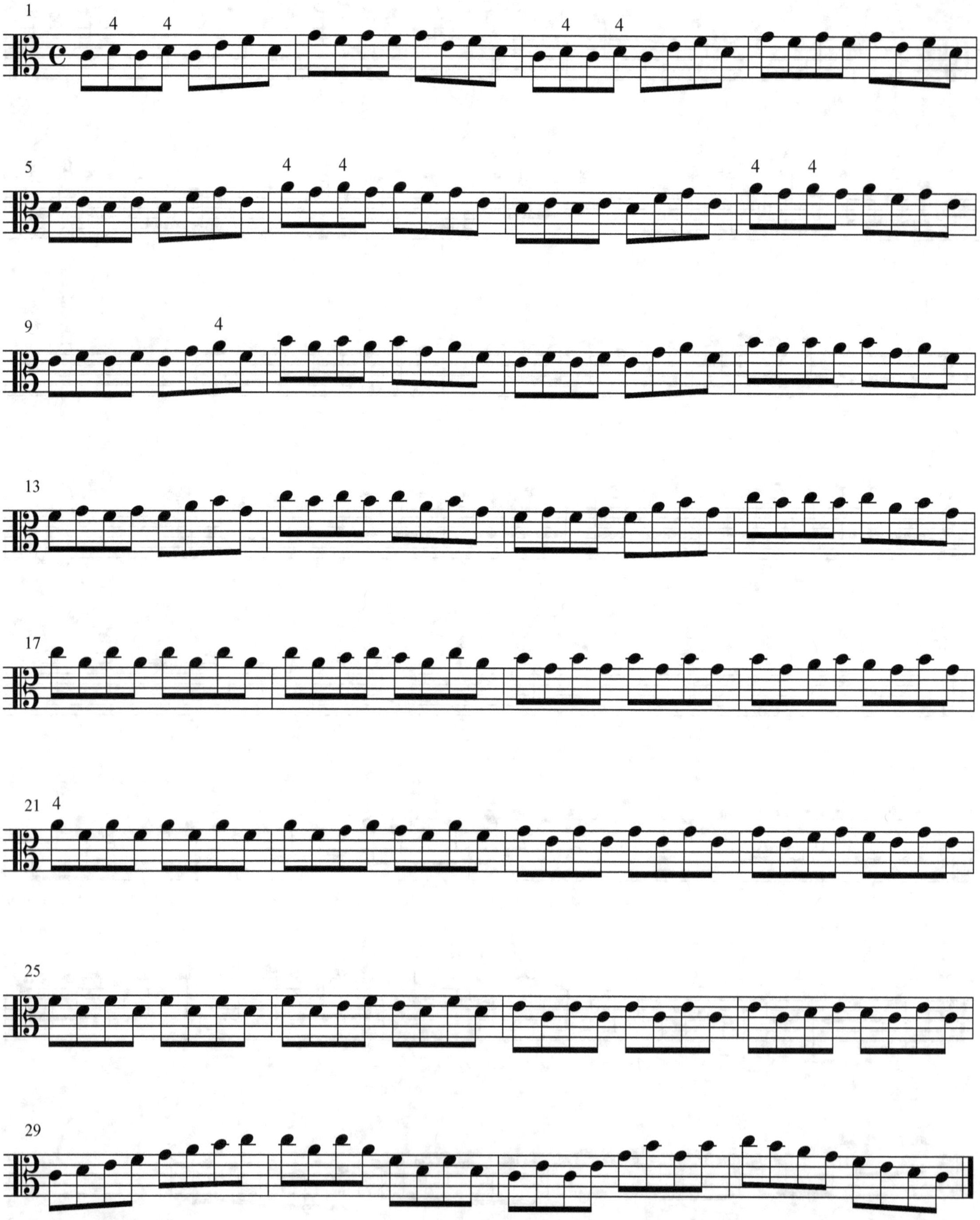

Grazioso (A)

Cimarosa, arr. Harvey

Finger Twister (B)

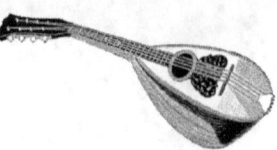

Warming Up for Viola, Book One

Grazioso (B)

Cimarosa, arr. Harvey

Warming Up for Viola, Book One

Variation (A)

Paganini, arr. Harvey

Daily Exercise (B)

Variation (B)

Paganini, arr. Harvey

41

©2004 C. Harvey Publications All Rights Reserved.

Warming Up for Viola, Book One

Finger Workout (A)

Allegro (A)

Paxton, arr. Harvey

Finger Workout (B)

Allegro (B)

Paxton, arr. Harvey

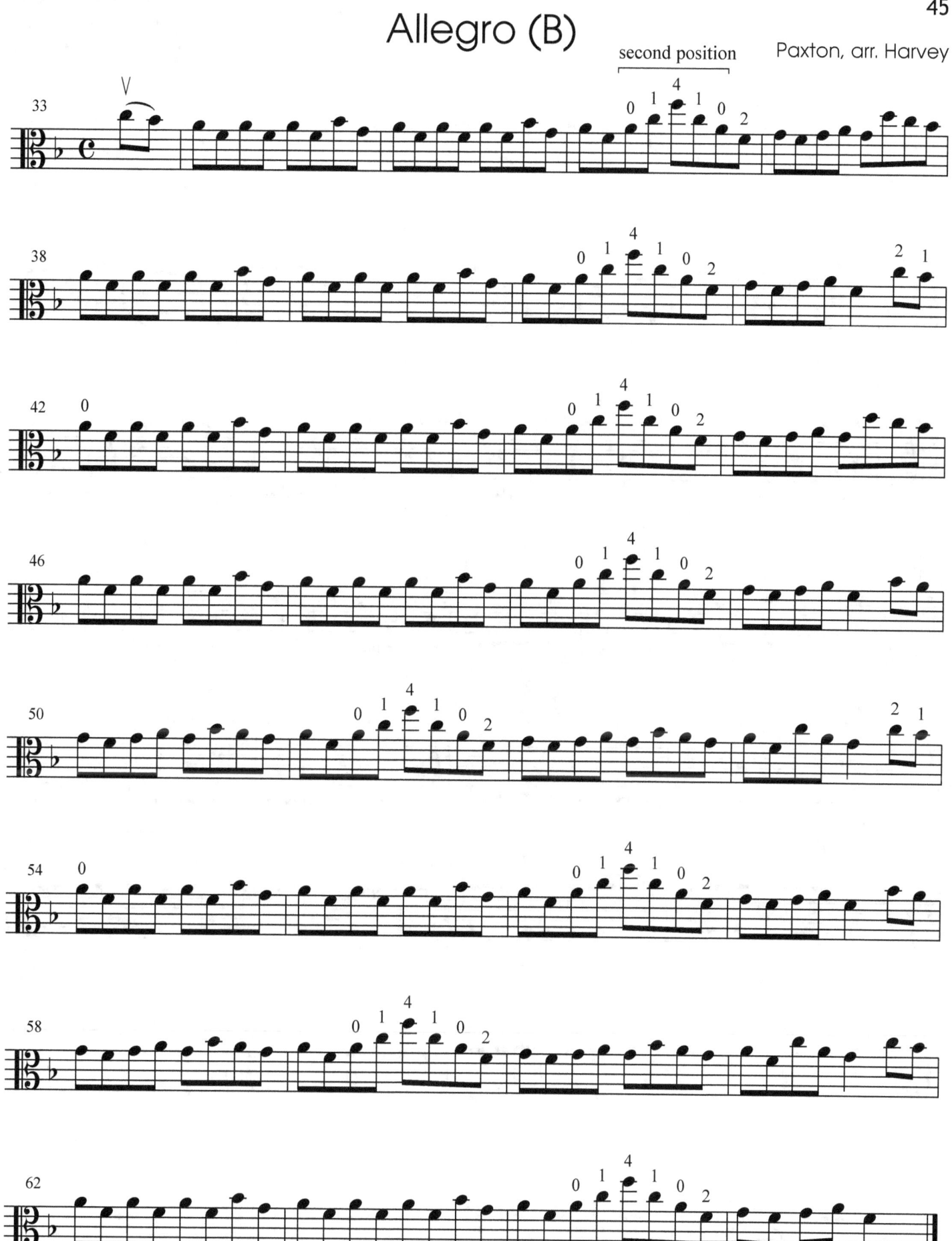

Finger Twister (A)

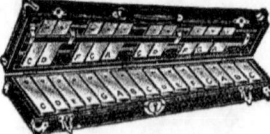

The Dashing Sergeant (A)

Trad., arr. Harvey

Finger Twister (B)

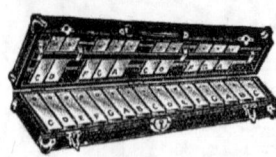

The Dashing Sergeant (B)

Trad., arr. Harvey

©2004 C. Harvey Publications All Rights Reserved.

Warming Up for Viola, Book One

available from **www.charveypublications.com**: CHP258

C Major Shifting for the Viola
1
Cassia Harvey

©2014 C. Harvey Publications All Rights Reserved.

www.ingramcontent.com/pod-product-compliance
Lightning Source LLC
Chambersburg PA
CBHW051424070526

44584CB00023B/3577